*Front endpaper:* A quartet of junior Gray Housecats. Gray fur and amber eyes are a classic combination.

*Front jacket:* A perfect example of a White Persian.

# CATS

*Above:* Bright, alert eyes, clean ears and nose, a full frill
and a soft, gleaming coat indicate a healthy, well
cared-for pet cat.

# CATS
## Angela Sayer

*Left:* almost identical twin tabbies, of no particular
breed, pose together on a sunlit windowsill. This tabby
coloring is the natural coat pattern of the domestic cat,
providing perfect camouflage in woodland shade. The
pattern typically shows a distinct "M" on the forehead,
lines running back from the eyes and heavy "necklace"
lines around the neck.

# Contents

*Left:* Two fairly rare Red and Cream Burmese kittens rest after a hectic play period. The coloring is a pale, creamy tangerine, with slight tabby markings on the face, back and tail but not on the sides and belly.

This book was devised and produced by Multimedia Publications (UK) Ltd

*Editor* **Richard Rosenfeld**
*Design* **Behram Kapadia**
*Picture Research* **Charlotte Deane**
*Production* **Arnon Orbach**

Copyright © Multimedia Publications (UK) Ltd

Published in this edition by Galley Press, an imprint of W. H. Smith and Son Limited, Registered No. 237811 England. Trading as WHS Distributors, St John's House, East Street, Leicester, LE1 6NE

ISBN 0-86136-767-7

Printed in Spain by Cayfosa, Barcelona
Dep. Legal B-30.100 - 1984

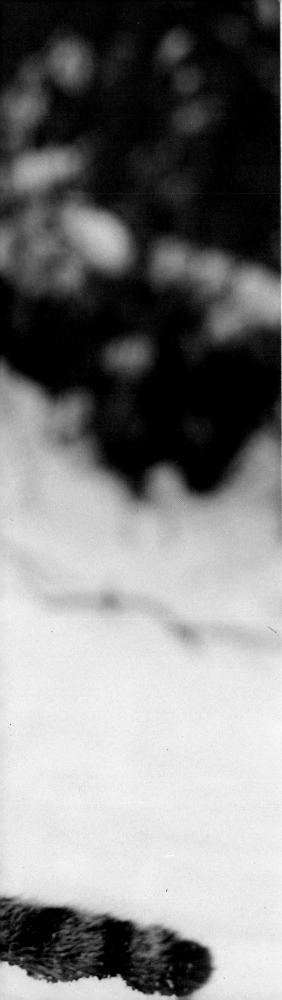

# Introduction

The cat possesses remarkable powers of survival and it is an extremely skilled and patient hunter. Its special retractile claws and sharp dentition provide it with lethal weapons and make it a perfect carnivore. It is as cautious as it is courageous and, despite more than three thousand years of domestication, the cat retains, just below the surface, the innate reactions and savage instincts of its ancestor *miacis*, which evolved during the age of the dinosaurs.

## Mother care

Cats mature early and are fertile. The female cat can produce litters of two to six kittens, two or three times a year, so it is easy to see how cats have spread and flourished world-wide.

The female cat is totally absorbed in the rearing of her litter and conscientiously feeds, washes and guards them at all times. She is loathe to leave her kittens even to feed or drink and if danger threatens will fight to the death to protect them.

Even after weaning, the mother cat still continues caring for her family, passing on to her offspring all the skills and routines that are necessary for them to enjoy a full and successful feline life. Domestic cats are usually left with their mothers until they are about 12 weeks old. Feral kittens stay longer, usually several months.

## Battle scars

Male cats are naturally solitary animals and rarely show any interest in their offspring. However, they are fierce fighters, quick to defend their mates and territorial boundaries. Feral toms often bear torn ears and other battle scars.

Most pet cats are neutered. This ensures that they lead contented lives, without displaying unsociable habits such as territorial marking, while retaining all their most admirable characteristics – independence, affection, cleanliness and companionship.

In the home, kittens can be great fun. They make wonderful companions, are very lively and playful and are a continuous delight, though they can also be extraordinarily mischievous! Their sharp little claws and teeth can damage furniture and clothes. They bear no resemblance to the adult, which is a much quicker, more relaxed creature.

*Left:* One of a breed of cats that has remained unchanged in size, shape, character or color for thousands of years, this sleek domestic tabby surveys the snow-clad landscape, alert for signs of possible prey. Note the distinctive, almost symmetrical markings, on the forehead, cheeks, legs and tail.

# Beautiful Kittens

A mother cat carries her kittens for a gestation period of 65 days (there will be no obvious sign that she is pregnant for the first 20 days or so), then gives birth to a litter or kindle of blind, deaf and furry youngsters. At first, the kittens spend their time sleeping and feeding from their mother while their eyes gradually open – around the third or fourth day in the Oriental breeds, and from 7 to 14 days in kittens of other varieties. At three weeks, kittens are able to stand and play; at four weeks they begin to explore beyond their nest.

## Feeding

At this time, the mother may encourage them to try some of the food she usually eats, and although they will continue to suckle until nine or ten weeks old, or even longer, the kittens soon learn to eat solid foods. They get their first set of teeth when only six weeks old. While the kittens feed only on milk, the mother licks away their excretions, but as soon as they start eating solids, they will need a litter box.

## Re-homing kittens

Pet cats generally have their kittens taken from them for re-homing at 10 or 12 weeks of age, while the feral mother will keep her kittens for several months, sharing the hunting and scavenging for food, and sleeping with them to provide warmth. This is because a kitten's dentition, muscular strength and skill are not sufficiently developed for full independence until it is six to nine months old.

The kitten removed to a new home needs lots of attention, affection, warmth and play opportunities to compensate for the loss of its mother and littermates. It requires feeding four or five times a day – always feed it in the same place – and must be regularly groomed to keep its coat in good condition. Its ears, eyes, teeth, claws and coat should be checked for cleanliness or signs of infection, and it will require vaccinations against the most serious of feline diseases, infectious enteritis and flu.

If it is confined to the home, the kitten will need a litter box and this should be kept clean. Unless it is to be bred from, the kitten should be neutered at around six months.

*Left:* A proud Chinchilla lavishes love, care and her undivided attention on her kitten. The Chinchilla is usually smaller than other long-haired breeds.

*Above:* The young kitten starts to explore beyond the nest from three to four weeks, and at six weeks is quite adventurous. Between periods of intense play it is inclined to roll over and rest wherever it happens to find itself. Like all small kittens, this tabby has blue colored eyes which will change to another color at weaning.

*Left:* The exploratory stage can be a dangerous one for the young kitten, which may easily roam far from the nest and meet unexpected hazards. This pretty, silver shaded, long-haired kitten has discovered the garden pool. Luckily, it has paused to examine its reflection, rather than tumbling in. Kittens need constant watching.

*Above:* A trio of pedigree Chinchilla kittens have their first experience of the fresh air and colorful beauty of a summer garden. Any tabby markings will disappear as they grow older.

*Left:* These eight-weeks-old Tonkinese kittens, posing with their year-old brother, were produced by mating together the closely related Burmese and Siamese breeds. The resulting offspring are midway between their parent breeds in coloring and temperament – very extrovert, affectionate and rather mischievous. They have dark-colored points, though less so than those of the Siamese and, generally, they have aquamarine-colored eyes.

*Left:* At the exploring age, kittens discover and test all types of materials for their play potential. Although the traditional concept of the kitten playing with a ball of yarn might seem particularly appealing, do beware. Today's man-made knitting yarns are tough and resilient. They may damage the kitten's teeth and are also dangerous if swallowed, so keep them stored out of reach.

*Right:* It is essential to introduce potential pet partners to one another at a young age, otherwise they may find it difficult to get along well when they are older. Do not, however, leave them alone together until they have accepted each other.

*Below:* Like all of the Himalayan breeds, the Birman has blue eyes; they change from baby blue to true blue at about six to eight weeks of age. The Birman is readily distinguished, however, by its striking snow-white "gloves" on all four paws.

*Above:* On its first expedition into the great outdoors a kitten is ever alert for new sights, sounds and stimuli, and uses every scrap of available cover for possible retreat. The eye-liner markings around this pretty kitten's eyes make them appear to be much larger than they actually are.

*Right:* Climbing is a natural attribute for the inquisitive kitten, who will take every opportunity of scaling trees and shrubs to obtain a better view of its surroundings.

*Below:* Even when her kittens are quite large and rapidly reaching the age of independence, the female cat is content to allow them to suckle. If they persist in suckling, however, keep them away from her – otherwise the necessary weaning process will become much more difficult.

*Above:* Long-haired kittens like this appealing cream one need a little extra care and attention in order to keep their soft coats in immaculate condition, and prevent the formation of "mats." Give them a thorough but gentle brushing every day.

16

*Above:* Short-haired kittens, like this sleepy young tabby, need very little grooming. A weekly brush and comb will remove dead hairs and keep the coat spotlessly clean. Also, it should be fine-textured and smooth, without any hint of wooliness.

*Left:* Prior to weaning, kittens are usually happy in most situations created by their owners, but this one is clearly distressed at being placed in a fruit bowl for its photographic session. Kittens always prefer warm, soft surfaces and are very responsive to gentle petting.

*Below:* This little Seal Colorpoint is showing a typically defensive attitude, turning sideways to its threatening adversary, fluffing up its tail and coat in order to look as large and menacing as possible, and hissing a warning.

*Above:* This tabby and white kitten enjoying its exercise in the spring sunshine is clearly a healthy one. Bright eyes, a clean and gleaming coat and an inquisitive, alert manner all point to its potential as the perfect feline pet.

*Above:* Feral kittens enjoy spending the daylight hours
playing together in safe, secluded spots near their
well-hidden nest site, while their mother is away
hunting or foraging for food.

*Above:* The hunting instinct is suppressed in the very
young kitten, so it is generally safe to introduce it to
animals and birds that will later be its natural prey – but
don't leave them together unsupervised.

*Left:* Farm kittens spend their weaning days romping and playing around the various barns, learning the hunting skills that they will be called upon to use as mature cats. Natural play behavior between siblings develops muscles and powers of coordination, preparing them for the time when they must become self-sufficient.

*Left:* Kittens brought up with horses and ponies in the farm-yard soon learn the elements of safety to be observed around large, heavy-hooved animals. Members of the horse family seem to have a natural affinity for the cat, who keeps down the numbers of rats and mice attracted to the grains.

*Above:* A trio of pedigree Ragdolls. This breed was
developed in the USA in the late 1960s. Their learning
processes are governed mainly by play and through
exploring the owner's home.

# Mischievous Cats

The cat's skeleton and muscle arrangement allow for great flexibility and agility, enabling it to climb and jump superbly. It is easily able to clear four or five times its own height from a crouching, stationary position and, when startled, is able to leap straight up in the air, landing to the side or behind its take-off point in an automatic, defensive measure. Climbing upward is fairly simple; the cat uses its strong hooked claws to cling, while its powerful hindleg muscles propel it upward. Jumping down is more complex, so the cat takes greater care, often converting a steep descent into two or three intermediate stages to reduce the potentially harsh impact on its forelegs.

**Safe landings**
Climbing down also presents problems, as the claws point in the wrong direction to be of any help. Most cats lower themselves down, rear-end first then, when near enough to the ground, perform a turning jump down, landing evenly on all four paws.

To ensure that it lands safely on its feet when it accidentally falls from a great height, the cat employs a sequence known as the self-righting reflex: muscles in the neck, chest, back, flanks and tail allow it to turn during a fall to land squarely on its paws, the impact cushioned by its flexed limbs and an arched spine.

**Territorial defense**
Free-ranging cats, whether neutered or entire, have distinct territories which they defend against intruders. This defense is usually achieved by psychological warfare, the cat scent-marking its boundaries by rubbing them with glands situated along its lips, above the eyes and at the root of its tail. Male cats also mark by urine-spraying.

Cats generally try to avoid physical confrontations, but when these do occur distinctive body language comes into play, first to warn off the intruder and, if this fails, to signal the opening stages of a fight. When cats do fight, it is a fierce and often very brief encounter, because feline teeth and claws inflict deep, serious wounds.

*Left:* The cat's natural agility and space perception enable it to perform both high and long jumps with remarkable ease, exceptional grace and surprising accuracy, often high above ground level. Its powerful spring is due to strong muscles in the back legs.

*Left:* This magnificent Russian Blue, in patroling its territory, has come upon an intruder and gives the preliminary signals of aggression – its coat stands up erect, its ears go back against the head, it turns sideways onto the marauder and begins to hiss in a threatening manner. This awe-inspiring sight is intended to frighten off the invader without actually fighting.

*Below:* A colony of feral cats visits the spot where a kind cat-lover brings them regular offerings of food. Although the cats are all equally hungry, they conform to a certain pattern of behavior in which the dominant animals eat first, a natural "pecking order" probably determined by inter-colony fighting.

*Above:* Pedigree and common cats climb with equal skill. They enjoy climbing trees and stropping (sharpening) their claws to remove dead scale and cuticle, against the roughness of the bark. To avoid damage to furniture and soft furnishings, you can buy or make a substitute scratching post for your cat, which can be kept indoors. It is an invaluable means of keeping cats in the best possible shape.

*Above:* This well-fed spotted tabby is obviously fascinated by the caged bird in the window, and is perhaps trying to work out how to procure it. The cat learns to be a hunter so, if you have other, vulnerable pets, keep them safely out of reach. Domestic cats never lose their savage instincts.

*Above:* These twin tabbies have seen a possible prey. They begin to hunt it down, starting with a stealthy stalk, then a running pounce with paws, claws and teeth ready to seize the quarry. But, contrary to popular belief, a cat does not instinctively kill to eat; that, in fact, is a learned response.

*Above:* Cats climb trees to hunt birds, escape from their
enemies and gain a good vantage point from which to
observe their own hunting grounds.

*Right:* This shows the typical defensive attitude of a frightened, cornered cat – head pulled into its shoulders to protect the throat, ears laid tightly back against the head, eyes narrowed to protect them from injury, and teeth bared in a fierce, hissing snarl. Along with these classic gestures of defiance, the cat also growls menacingly, even though it is frightened.

*Below:* All cats like to burrow inside objects which are apparently too small to contain them, and if these objects make crackling or rustling noises, so much the better! This happy, playful kitten has found the ideal toy – a tough, crumpled paper bag into which it barely fits, and which rustles excitingly with his every move.

*Above:* The conveniently spaced branches of a pine tree make a natural ladder for a young White Short-hair as it attempts, unsuccessfully, to reach a tempting nest of wood pigeon fledglings.

*Above:* Animals cannot perceive color in the same way as man. Ginger or orange-red appears as the same gray tone as green, so this bright tabby is naturally camouflaged from any other feline aggressor.

*Above:* The free-ranging cat, whether pedigree or pet, spends a great deal of pleasurable time in checking out its territory, sniffing at plants for the scent of other cats.

The sense of smell is highly developed and plays an important part in sexual identification as well as in establishing territorial marking.

*Right:* Farm cats are generally raised alongside the other animals and birds with which they must learn to coexist during adulthood. It is important that they understand the difference between friends and foes. Although this ginger cat would confidently tackle a wild bird of equal size, he is relaxed and happy with this cockerel.

*Below:* These White Short-hair kittens are expected to live in complete harmony with their owner's guinea pigs, and so receive early lessons in good relations. The guinea pig has no fear of the cats and makes no attempt to run away, when the kittens could be tempted to give chase. It is important to watch your pets carefully at this stage.

*Above:* This kitten is merely following its natural liking for squeezing into snug-fitting, comfortable places to rest. He has discovered that the contours of the typewriter's keys fit his own shape to perfection.

36

*Right:* Dogs and cats, if introduced to one another at an early age often grow up to become inseparable friends like this Lhasa Apso and his ginger and white pal. They sleep, play and romp together, share the best chair and even eat from the same dish. While such a relationship is developing it is important to give both pets equal attention.

*Below:* Cats spend much of their resting time asleep and have the ability to fall instantly into a deep refreshing "catnap" wherever they happen to be. This comfort-loving tabby has chosen a safely secluded place in the flowerbed, hidden from danger by sheltering ferns.

# On Show

Pedigree cats come in two basic body types. The first is heavy-boned and chunky, with a large round head, huge round eyes, a short stub nose and tiny ears. The second is light-boned, long, lithe and elegant, with a long fine head, almond or oriental eyes, a long nose and large pointed ears. There are also two basic coats: long and flowing or short and fine. Curled coats are found only in specific breeds.

### Long- and short-hairs

When the long, full coat is found in conjunction with the heavy-boned body conformation, the cats are known as Persians or Long-hairs, and are generally named according to the color: the Black Persian, the Blue Persian and so on.

When a short coat is found in conjunction with the heavy-boned type, the cats are known as Short-hairs and, depending on their country of origin and certain features developed through careful breeding, may be classed as British, American, European or Exotic Short-hairs. Natural mutations in the Short-hair produced the tailless Manx cat and the Scottish Fold with its curled-over ears.

### Orientals

Cats of exaggerated light conformation, with very fine short coats are known as the Oriental Short-hairs. This group includes the well-known Siamese, renowned for its typically blue eyes and the way in which its coat color appears only on the extremities of its body – its "points." Oriental cats also appear in a wide range of colors and patterns including spotted, and shades such as silver.

Cats of less extreme structure and fine coats are called Foreign Short-hairs. They include the Abyssinian, Burmese, Korat and Russian Blue. Similar cats but with long fur are called Semi-Long-hairs. They include the Somali, Balinese, Turkish, Angora and Birman.

### Curly-coated

There are two main types allowed on the show bench – the Cornish and the Devon Rex. Although both were discovered in neighboring districts of England in the 1950s and 1960s, their distinct curled coats proved to be due to two different genes, so they are treated as separate breeds.

*Left:* A magnificent Smoke Persian wanders through the snow-clad garden, insulated by his silky coat. The copper-colored eyes are characteristic of this breed.

*Above:* Persian cats, like this pedigree Orange-eyed
White, have round faces, round eyes, stub noses,
strong chins and small ears set well apart. The ruff of
longer hair is also characteristic.

*Right:* Two cats of similar type but quite different breeds. On the left of the picture is a Blue Colorpoint or Himalayan, a true Persian cat of Siamese pattern and with the blue eyes characteristic of all Himalayan cats. On the right sits a Chinchilla Persian, each hair of its white coat lightly tipped with black, giving a silver effect.

*Right:* During the 1950s an unusual kitten with a curled coat was born in Cornwall, England, sired by an unknown male cat to a domestic pet queen. From these unlikely beginnings, the Cornish Rex breed has been developed, and now these elegant cats with curled coats are popular throughout the world in every coat, color and pattern.

*Above:* Cats of opposite type. On the left is a Foreign Lilac Short-hair, long and elegant with green eyes. On the right is a Blue Cream Persian, round and chunky with dark orange eyes.

*Right:* Although not the true type desired for the show bench, this strikingly colored Blue-Point Siamese has a beautiful pale coat as required by the show standard, and really excellent eye color. All Siamese cats should have deep, vivid sapphire blue eyes.

*Left:* A Seal-Point Siamese tom enjoying his exercise in the garden. Known originally as the Royal Cat of Siam, the first of these cats were brought out of Siam toward the end of the nineteenth century, and despite the frailty of the earliest kittens, soon became very popular.

*Right:* The White Oriental is Siamese in everything but coat color and may, in fact, be considered a Siamese cat in a white overcoat. For show purposes, its conformation is exactly the same as the Siamese, and its eye color should be equally intense. It is an affectionate, energetic, intelligent breed.

45

*Above:* The Tortoiseshell-and-White Long-hair, or
Calico Persian, has bright patches of red and black on
her white coat and show judges prefer to see a blaze of
color down the nose.

*Above:* The Devon Rex, seen here in a pure white specimen, is a rare breed of cat which has a curly coat. A Devon Rex makes an amusing and intelligent pet. It was first accepted as a separate breed in 1967.

*Above:* The Abyssinian is thought to be one of the most ancient of all feline breeds, although its history is not clearly documented. This variety is called Brown or Ruddy. The best Abyssinian show cats have no white body marks, although a white chin, as sported by this cat, is quite acceptable.

*Right:* At the cat show the judge examines each exhibit to determine how closely it conforms to an official standard of points. A separate standard is written for each breed, and describes such criteria as body shape, head shape, eye color, coat color, pattern and length as well as the overall appearance of the perfect specimen, including physical condition, presentation and size.

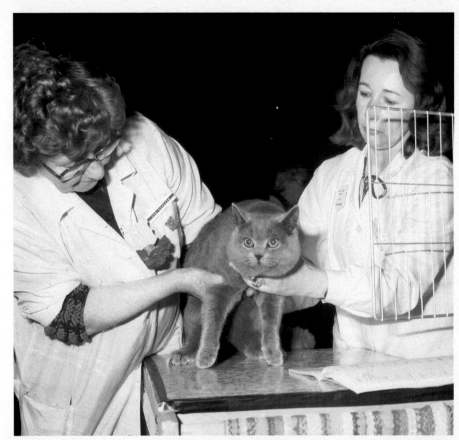

*Below:* Self or solid-colored Persian cats are found in a range of colors which includes black, blue (as here), chocolate, lilac, red, cream and white. The White Persian is found in three sub-varieties, named according to their eye color which may be orange or copper, blue and odd-eyed – one eye being orange or copper, the other blue.

*Above:* One of the most striking of the tabby
Long-haired cats is the breed called the Silver Tabby
Persian, which has a clear silver undercoat overlaid
with tabby markings in black. Although the classic
tabby bars, stripes and whorls are slightly blurred by
the long coat, the overall effect is striking.

*Right:* This attractive kitten is of the Persian variety known as the Bi-Color, in which at least half the coat is colored and the rest is white. Symmetrical markings are preferred by show judges, but this kitten would not be harshly penalized for having an off-set white blaze on his nose.

*Right:* The Cream Colorpoint, or Himalayan Persian, is a true Persian cat with Siamese coloring. It was developed by judicious crossbreeding, then careful selection for certain characteristics among each successive generation until the desired breed was achieved. All Himalayan cats have blue eyes.

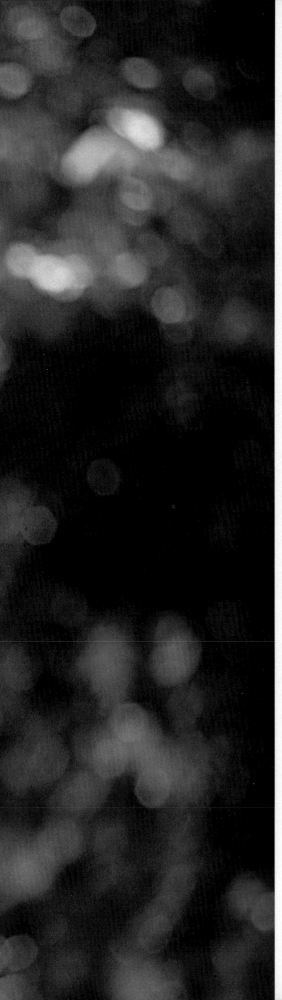

# In the Wild

All cats belong to the same sub-order of the Carnivora family, which divides into three groups: *Felis*, *Panthera* and *Acinonyx*. Felis and panthera are subdivided by species, while Acinonyx has only one member, the Cheetah.

There are 31 species in the genus Felis, but of these only *Felis catus*, the domestic cat, is found world-wide, having accompanied man on his explorations.

## Erosion of the environment

All members of the cat family are well equipped for survival in the normal course of evolutionary events, but some species have become extinct, or are threatened with extinction due to the greed and carelessness of man.

The cats most at risk are those with beautifully patterned pelts, which are much in demand for the fur trade.

Other species become threatened as their natural habitat is destroyed and the land developed for human use. The cats' natural prey disappears, they lose their natural cover, and gradually their environment is eroded away. Some specimens are killed, others move into alien territory to live out their lives in solitude; the species is doomed.

Pesticides also take their toll by getting into the lower levels of the food chain, and being gradually elevated into the diet of the carnivore, reducing or destroying fertility.

## African and Asian cats

The beautiful and endangered small cats include Africa's Golden Cat, Black-Footed Cat and the Serval; plus those also found in Asia – the African Wild Cat, the Caracal, the Jungle Cat and the Sand Cat.

The following are confined to Asia: the Bay Cat, Chinese Fishing Cat, Flat-Headed Cat, Iriomote Cat, Leopard Cat, Marbled Cat, Pallas's Cat, Rusty-Spotted Cat, and Temminck's Golden Cat. The Americas are rich in Bobcat, Geoffrey's Cat, Jaguarundi, Kodkod, Margay, Mountain Cat, Ocelot, Pampas Cat, Puma and the Tiger Cat. Only the Spanish Lynx is confined to Europe. The European Wild, or Forest Cat, is found also in Asia, and the Northern Lynx – native of Europe – is also found in Asia and America.

*Left:* The Ocelot, one of the world's most beautiful cats was brought to the brink of extinction, hunted and killed to make fur coats.

*Above:* The Cheetah is in a feline class all its own because it has only partially retractile claws, although it purrs like the smaller cats. Here, a female accompanied by her cubs drink at a waterhole.

*Above:* The Lynx's fur is dense in winter, thin in summer. It is a superb hunter and survives in a variety of barren and hostile environments. Always wily and cautious, it stays well clear of man.

*Above:* The Margay, or Long-tailed Spotted Cat, is a
South American species which closely resembles the
Ocelot. The Margay is a forest dweller, a superb
climber and, therefore, able to hunt among the
branches of tall trees, feeding on birds, lizards and
tree-frogs. Like the Ocelot, the Margay's numbers
have been decimated by pelt-hunters.

*Right:* The young Forest Wildcat may easily be mistaken for a domestic tabby, although its behavior when approached soon dispels that notion. The species is found in rocky mountain terrain, as well as in forest woodland, and occasional sightings of lone animals are made in various regions of Europe. The wildcat feeds on game birds, rabbits and other small mammals.

*Below:* The Cheetah is the fastest animal over short distances. It can easily run down its prey, which it kills by strangulation. It is rare for a Cheetah to tackle a full-grown zebra, however, and this cat may well be going for the mare's foal, off-camera. The Cheetah has become extinct in several original habitats.

*Left:* The Golden Cat of Africa is one of the rarest of all wild felines. It inhabits high deciduous forest areas and hunts at night, in the twilight and early dawn, feeding on birds, small mammals and small species of antelope like the Duiker, which it is thought to attract by imitating its call.

*Below:* This appealing Cheetah cub is slowly shedding the long, woolly mantle of bluish-gray fur which covers its spotted pattern. It helps the young animal to remain disguised in the bush while its mother hunts. This mantle slowly reduces to a slight mane at 10 weeks and at three months the dark undercoat becomes tawny.

*Right:* The Jungle Cat is one of the species favored by the Ancient Egyptians, who used it as a hunting cat to catch water birds in the reed beds of the Nile. Larger than the Forest Wildcat, the Jungle Cat has long legs and a ticked tawny coat, resembling that of an Abyssinian.

*Below:* Pallas's Cat, or the Manul, differs from the domestic cat in the structure of its eyes. In the domestic cat, dilated pupils form a slit, while in the Manul, the pupil aperture is round. Slightly larger than the domestic cat, the Manul makes sounds like a dog yapping and an owl hooting. Its natural habitat is Central Asia.

*Above:* A beautiful young Ocelot refreshes itself at a
river bank in Venezuela. During daylight hours,
Ocelots are usually tucked away under cover of forest
and bushland.

*Right:* The handsome Leopard Cat is the commonest wildcat in southern Asia. Its natural habitat is forest and jungle at various levels, from lowland to high mountains. A solitary species, it hunts mainly at night and preys on jungle fowl, small mammals and young deer, fish and reptiles.

*Below:* A pair of Ocelots kept at the Arizona-Sonora Desert Museum, live in an environment designed to encourage them to behave naturally and breed regularly. Such captive breeding pairs enable gene pools of endangered species to be protected so that rare animals can be saved from extinction.

*Left:* The very rare, nocturnal Marbled Cat, found in the thick forests of Nepal and eastward to Sumatra, is slightly larger than the domestic cat with small, rounded ears and a long, thick and bushy tail. Its tawny coat is dappled with large, irregular blotches of dark brown edged with black.

*Below:* The South American Margay differs from the Ocelot, in being smaller and more slimly built. It stands higher on its legs and has a longer tail. Its spots are generally darker in the center than those of the Ocelot and form longitudinal rows. The name Margay, or Marguey, can be translated as tiger cat, in reference to its ferocity.

*Right:* The Scottish Wildcat is large, stocky and almost impossible to tame. Very rare in its native habitat, having been ruthlessly hunted as vermin early in this century, numbers increased during recent years and occasional sightings are now made. The Wildcat hunts large birds and small mammals.

*Below:* Named after the *pajero* or high pampas grass of the area of Argentina in which it is found, the Pampas Cat is about the same size as the Wildcat. Its coloring is very variable, ranging from yellowish-white to gray, with bands of yellow or brown running from the back to the flanks, sometimes forming blotches and bars.

*Above:* A young Serval, perhaps the most graceful of the African cats. It inhabits high grass, scrub and reed beds, living close to water. The Serval's prey includes birds, lizards, snakes and small animals. Its coat is yellowish with black markings.

## Picture Credits

*Back endpaper:* Red Self kittens, a longhaired breed developed from the Red Tabby. Large copper eyes and small pointed ears are typical of this breed.

*Back jacket:* A ginger housecat keeping lookout from the safety of a tree stump.